The Tears of Things

Poems

The Tears of Things

Poems

Catherine Hamrick

MADVILLE
PUBLISHING
LAKE DALLAS, TEXAS

Copyright © 2025 by Catherine Hamrick
All rights reserved
Printed in the United States of America

FIRST EDITION

Requests for permission to reprint or reuse material from this work
should be sent to:

Permissions
Madville Publishing
PO Box 358
Lake Dallas, TX 75065

Cover Photo: Juliana Nan, licensed through Shutterstock
Author Photo: Alex Ruble

ISBN: 978-1-963695-11-3 paperback
978-1-963695-12-0 ebook
Library of Congress Control Number: 2024939446

*In memory of my parents and for Dan,
who guided the way to finding my voice*

Contents

Winter

Iowa Dreams	1
Midwinter Insomniac	2
Fat Tuesday Freeze	3
Second Chance Crack-up	4
Night of the Insistent Moon	6
Origami Storm	7
Origins of the World in a Greenhouse	9
Lithium Unplugged	10
Lenten Roses	12
Through Irish Eyes	13

Spring

642 Square Feet (Apartment Therapy)	17
House Finches	19
Dwarf Iris Blessing	21
Fauve Crocuses	22
Detached	23
Before Dogwood Winter	25
Death on a Sidewalk	26
Never a Moonlit Lie	27
My Father on D-Day and Mountain Shade	28

Summer

Swimming After Trout	33
Central Florida Postcard	34
Chattahoochee: Songs I Never Heard till Now	35
Coneflower Sequence	37
Peach Heat: Out of Hand	38
Deception	39

Nowhere Duet	40
The Shadow of My Father's Beard	41
Immersion	43
Summer Contained	44

Fall

Opening to Your Dark Eye	47
Royal Wind Riders	48
The New Orange	50
Around the Corner	51
Apple Chill	53
Blue Ridge Weather Report	54
October Martini	55
Persimmon Surrender	56
Autumn Coda, Winter Wondering	57

The Fifth Season

Birdwatch	61
Song on a Winter's Day	62
When You Need a Chat with Jesus	64
what's more	66
At Sunrise: Metta Meditation	68
Acknowledgments	70
Notes	72
About the Author	73

Winter

Iowa Dreams

December rose raw and sunless; layers piled roadside gray
where plows threw snow, sand, and ice in gritty drifts

packed down into rough-hewn walls my shovel could not breach.
Christmas carols rang foreign; the birdbath brimmed with stone water.

My dreams rolled Midwest—May prairies greening
and sod breaking in rectangular patches

and my neighbor warning that cucumber seeds never burrowed
until Mother's Day when peonies flirted in ruffled skirts.

The cold crept me awake, and I took a bundled turn
in the neighbor's garden; my glove-dimmed fingers unlatched

the cypress moon gate, concrete foo dogs grimacing
on either side as blue hollies pricked the night blanket.

Woody vines weighted the arbor's bones,
and river birches peeled salmon in the side yard

where needle-thin bird tracks ghosted—
a temple bell chimed copper prayers,

and I plunged boot-deep back to my deck and stopped
to brush off the fishnet metal top of Nannie's patio table

that once baked on Georgia lemonade days. The wind had rounded
the snow in the laps of the ice-cream chairs, now her plump bridge foursome

greedy for the triumph of sweeping pennies into leather coin purses
that snapped shut, smartly enough, with kiss clasps—

and I longed for iron-worn bedsheets billowing in cumulus
motion on a clothesline as my father staked bean poles

in crooked clay rows and bent to plant Kentucky Wonders
before Good Friday thundered in the Appalachian foothills.

Midwinter Insomniac

The sun's sleeping spree,
two weeks behind cloud cover,
leaves me staring down the face
that ticks motherless dogs to calm

but keeps me wound up—
the back of my eye sockets
burned out and wet howls
gone the way of dry heaves.

They say insomnia kills off
twelve years, and I've counted them
down, sliding into warm baths,
buzzing my brain with Benadryl,

picking the skin off scalded milk,
sipping lavender-chamomile tea,
whistle of the kettle
shrilling the alarm of dawn

swallowing night, and I turn,
on one side and then the other,
a pillow between my knees
bent at ninety degrees, my hands

clasped in the marble prayer
of an effigy, exhausting
appeals then falling
into a doze brushed

by the wings of a dragonfly,
textured like stained glass.
It hovers above the flat-topped
seed pod of a mud-risen lotus

and sizzles the air to turn
heart wheels with a mate—
until the furnace bangs,
killing the somersaulting flight.

Fat Tuesday Freeze

On an errand
to the woodpile,
I, snow angel,
fell from grace,
slick-tripped
on ice-sheeted
green moss rock.

The wind froze.

You, Mardi Gras baby,
concrete cherub
draped with gold, green,
and purple beads,
stood dead
except for the hint
of your smirk.

Second Chance Crack-up

I feared crossing bay bridges on dark nights
that blinded us to land unless shore lights

winked, like starshine, hinting of miles to cross
over water rippling murky—so I held on

to a banged-up Corolla that allowed for
cranking down the windows (even in seasons

of cold teeth) in case of an accidental plunge,
until he bought a convertible with push buttons.

"Done," he said with the trouble of it all,
forgetting he once doted on the charm

of my hang-up; early infatuation has
the habit of excusing the irrational

until late irritation kills it. The sunroof
of a Honda Civic was our window

to winter hunts for Orion's belt—what thrills
at thirty glitters hard at forty: we had chased

a dead man's tale, numb to February's sting
in the temporary heat of "forever."

Three-and-a-half sleeping pills past 4 a.m.,
I slipped out of bed, my head still hammered

by our argument, though the air did not stir
except for flutters brushing his throat.

I snatched up an unfinished dreamcatcher,
tying off yarn tails with gold stars

and crescent moons as cunning
as miniature cookie cutters.

There's no truth to the moon—only a cratered face
without atmosphere to burn meteor hits.

I dropped the dreamcatcher for the hum
that would disappear me to the nowhere

forbidden by DSM-IV magicians
who dispensed green pills that dispatched me,

on lucky nights, to dreamless lands until dawn
broke, thoughts roller-coasting

like 4-D rides dropping headfirst, shooting up,
and spiraling off like nonstop fireworks.

The last trick was on me, so I slammed
myself inside the convertible, leaned in

to turn the key, and reclined, inhaling
four counts, holding four, exhaling six,

holding two—then again—the breath of life
on slow repeat, waiting for drowsiness

to cloud the clock blazing annoyance
with the flip of yellow minutes . . .

I spun the dial, hunting a public radio tune:
Where the hell was Mozart's *Requiem Mass*?

No one should die to BBC radio drone,
but that's all you get on Greenwich Mean Time.

The engine rattled, and I cut the motor,
cracking up at my second chance—

the absurdity of a ragtop, in a drafty garage,
with a broken window, at daybreak.

Night of the Insistent Moon

Winter's beat went arrhythmic, and I lost
count to rain crystals pattering panes,

to wordless chatter clicking my teeth,
to the titmouse's peter-peter-peter

pecking my brain, and I burned to unpack sanity
from a lightbox, to drift in the velvet

of blackout panels, to tuck hospital corners
in my mother's crisp practice, now her lost art.

Nightly at nine o'clock, I dispensed benzos,
doling out haphazard naps until I swallowed

a hangover's worth; meting out sleep
stops you from saving up for a dead end.

On a windless night, great horned owls stuttered hoots
to the insistent moon squeezing between blinds,

and I opened to the gaze of the shadow man,
as if tuning to the slow pull

of a sonorous cello tone, mellowing
to that ancient call—the tears of things.

Origami Storm

1

The domestic engineer of measured cups,
my mother teaspooned chocolate chip dough

in same-size circles on scarred cookie sheets
and edited recipes in cookbook margins,

noting, "Cooking is chemistry."
The wielder of pinking shears zigzagging

on the bias of sensible school-dress cloth,
she freshened a black-and-white-checked

hand-me-down with pearl buttons and adorned
the pockets with ebony rickrack.

I scratched at crinolines, irritated
that she lacked the artistry to cut,

fold, and string origami cranes
from the dining room chandelier,

a storm of wings shadowing walls
washed in rainbows of antique prisms.

"A flock of one thousand promises happiness,"
said my teacher during the unit on Japan.

2

Autumn closed into winter, and her hands
lost the habit of clipping oakleaf hydrangeas

past their prime; praise for the papery
flowers with tints of sunset

and the roll of their Latin name
went dead on her tongue; she mismatched

mornings with ice cream for breakfast,
floral blouses paired with plaid pants,

prayer that greeted God with hello,
ended with bye-bye and a wave.

She took to wearing her sweater
turned inside out and backwards,

tugging at the tag while lisping
the ABC song we once sang

with her face close to mine as she soaped
and rinsed my hands while I tiptoed

on a stepstool, the fortune
of one thousand cranes in my grasp.

Origins of the World in a Greenhouse

An orchid spikes purple
at daybreak; ruched wings
drop me headfirst,
speckled, sticky, and noisy,
in a hothouse crowd—I gasp,
groping for the next curve,
and my mother unwilts
with the upturn of her mouth.

Noon is lunchtime, but she refuses
to sit, wandering in middle age,
like a clockwork doll,
dotting lipstick on her Cupid's bow
and lower lip then coloring
inside the lines and inner
corners, ready for my father's
return—six hours too soon.

At dusk, my voice can't
get through, like a signal
interrupted and distorted
before reaching a satellite
radio tuner—with the hiss
of partial cancellation;
sundown agitation kills
the scent of moonflowers.

Lithium Unplugged

I scheduled an appointment, hands shaking,
after a pent-up storm, like a shelf cloud

pressing on eastern cottonwoods,
broke and emptied out.

The first doctor, a round-chinned Irishman,
Boston-born and Harvard-trained, poked

among ancestral tales: brooding classics scholars,
the great-great something-or-other suicide,

and my grandfather losing weekends to binges
on Poe, Camels, silence, and drink.

Family history as semi-mute as British headstones
over-rubbed by tourists and my desperation

for normalcy rendered an end-of-session
judgment: you'll carry lithium to your grave.

This precious metal came cheap, so I bought
into silver-bullet promises promoting

gold-standard treatment and, wishing hard
for the idea of order, pulled at puppet strings,

measuring speech, restraining gesture,
always checking for the face in the front row

detecting a twitch in my lucid-eyed charm.
The cocktail hour (party of one) started

at 7 a.m., with two-ingredient recipes
(lithium plus antidepressant)

coming and going like random fog,
and I latched onto orange-bottled hope

and monikers with quick linguistic twists
that would stick to my tongue and brain,

as clever as paint-chip names promising
a mood to color a kitchen or bedroom.

The novelty wore off as the years blurred on,
a white-coat parade praising

my resume while they tinkered and tested
and I faked control of two-faced theater.

There's no poetry in waiting rooms hung
with big-box art hinting at indigo forests

and misty seascapes—just tapping, tics, tremors,
whispers, and the crinkle of magazine pages.

Untouched by fire, I shunned myth remaking:
soaring just for the burn of wax on the neck

and a blink in the sun's eye (glory paid for
by a plunge in the sea)—this was no way to die.

"This is no way to live," said the umpteenth doctor,
who shuffled in after loitering for a smoke;

hunched over and pecking two-fingered notes,
he unplugged the element mined to power

phones, tablets, and electric cars before it killed
my kidneys, and I packed up and crated

the cat—southbound for gardens where blush
camellias cling through winter then downturn,

bell-like and ruffled with golden rot, dropping
petal by petal on pine straw-punctured beds.

Lenten Roses

The Christmas rose opened, but I went
dormant in the season of his last hope,
fleeing at Epiphany—hinting at return.
"Keep faith," I said, "for Lenten roses."

He called, saying he missed the habit of me.

Their lances mounded low, promise bedded,
evergreen. At night I shut the phone
in a sock drawer, but still proffered maybe.
"Keep faith," I emailed, "for Lenten roses."

He sent a card, saying he missed midnight firelight.

February rattled the beech, littering
autumn's leavings. I slipped his note
in the junk mail drawer, still tendering maybe.
"Keep faith," I emailed, "for Lenten roses."

He left a voicemail, saying he wouldn't wait.

Sawtooth blades cut hard-freeze snow, and blooms
pushed up, downward shy, nodding blush—
but I stayed mute, and Lent gave me up,
without penance, prayer, or devotion.

He emailed, saying he donated my down coat—

and cleaned out ashes overwintering
in the fireplace, cleared swifts from the chimney,
and settled for the ease of gas logs, done
with fire starters and wood, soot and stains.

Through Irish Eyes

My father said, "Superstition doesn't serve,"
so I never scrounged the ground
for a four-leaf clover during recess
to stow a bit of Father, Son,
Holy Ghost—plus grace—in my pocket,
but lounged in the outfield
and laced daisy chains, hopeful
no softball would plop my way.

But this St. Patrick's Day, I stomp
an icy puddle and misspell
my name—Cait catches my fancy.
The beach at dusk is wet with clouds,
like smoky puffs, and my depression
runs wild with joy as the tide washes
out, leaving silvery pools, like footprints
shimmering on burnt charcoal.

I take whisky neat from a Kildare
tumbler, and my hazel eyes turn green.

Spring

642 Square Feet (Apartment Therapy)

The duck-and-huddle of the Atomic Age drove my parents
underground to build a cement-block bomb shelter

with a hollow-door shield against Castro's fierce beard—
a helter-skelter haven for hoarding chipped furniture,

baluster vases, and piles of *Life* and *Look* that fanned
the walnut veneer of their Early American coffee table.

Mom wedged ranch unchic into that fallout tumble
after family heirlooms turned up at her door.

She had the good sense to mix Chinese Chippendale
end tables, Canton blue china, and Hiroshige

harbor prints with Middle Tennessee antiques
and coin silver shadowboxed against charcoal felt.

Fifty-plus years wore down the familiar:
the dent of my father's head in the sofa pillow,

threads snagged and loosened on my mother's easy chair,
a settling, like the creak of a Windsor rocker.

My possessions accumulate fewer by the year,
odds and ends to fit into 642 square feet.

He claimed red, green, and gold ornaments
and fairy lights strangling newspaper rolls,

sweeping aside blue and pearl notions—the year
Christmas hijacked Hanukkah on a designer's whim.

The bronze teardrop tree topper stayed, boxed
and bubble-wrapped, a January-sale leftover.

What is it to be a professional packer,
the automaton sorter of broken houses—

without the squabbles of this-is-mine-not-yours-it-went-on-
my-charge-card-and-I-saw-that-painting-in-Paris-first?

Am I brave enough to stroke the tiger stripes
of a quarter-sawn oak library table, where I will dine,

going against the grain that mahogany is more tasteful?
This leave-taking lacks elegance, with abbreviated

journeys around my room, yet my heirs will thank me
for the U-Haul load downsized four decades early.

House Finches

The time between seasons finishes itself—twitters bursting into equinox chatter and spring peeper one notes slurring upward and woodpeckers drilling an urgency that possesses me to buy Boston ferns to hang from the balcony, as if I can fill in a memory bare spot, like the bank of windows in my mother's den with iron brackets jutting from the frame, where she hung baskets waterfalling fronds—"nature's curtain," she said.

As I stand at the window, the far-right fern trembles, and a bird streaked grayish brown darts past her mate perched on the cathedral trellis steadied in a planter. His head tilts from right to left and back again, with warbles jumping down the scale, as bright as his tomato-spattered cap, pulsing throat, and breast, except for harsh notes punctuating here and there—fluffing feathers, he bathes in sunlight.

In the flirt of a warm spell, I surrender the basket to the season's first clutch and settle into the give of an antique wicker chair starting to tatter and toss offerings of coco fiber and curls swept up after a trim, but the birds are wary, returning only when I close the door. The male, in a defiant moment, lights on the railing and throws back his head and sings, throat throbbing and beak half-open while balancing a pine-straw needle.

I yield the balcony, lifting a sheer to study the delivery of stems, grasses, rootlets, and leaves to the female fluttering, weaving, and tamping down the nest. Days slide by, pollen dusting gummy green and sapping my energy until chirps, like a squeaking wheel, break my coffee-musing silence—and I rise to spy on the male regurgitating in his mate's mouth, and she turns, dipping to feed the hatchlings.

I resist the urge to sneak outside, climb a stepladder, and part the browning fronds to peep at the nestlings—clumsy and huddling like a multicell mass, with down wisps and dark globe eyes like superhero masks and necks stretching up and heads wobbling and mouths opening, eager and pink. Digging out my father's binoculars, I drag a dining chair to the window and resume my watch, standing on the saddle seat.

Within two weeks, the boldest takes to perching at the edge of the nest, tail up, breast puffing, and eyes glittering—like Washington crossing the Delaware, so I name him George. He flaps, hungry and impatient, ruffling what's left of the leaves, then taps a dance and leaps from the crowd squawking, pushing, and piling on each other, flailing their wings until stepping off to test the air with short flights and return hops before scattering.

I remove the nest sagging from the weight of a fecal-sac wreath—the cup measuring three inches wide and deep—and wonder whether my hair softened the finches' first days. After spritzing the ferns with an olive-oil-and-garlic concoction, I pot a new plant, sprinkle it with baking soda, and sleep with the windows unlatched for mourning dove coos and the swish and gurgle of coffee percolating before my mother pours a cup for porch sitting.

Dwarf Iris Blessing

Blue-violet tongues
sing, rapture swelling,
toned with plum speckles,
titanium blotches,
and yellow-flame licks,
leaves like grass,
spring's early lawn—
a green amen.

Fauve Crocuses

This March madness plays tug of war
between icy dips and warm rises

that tease me to walk abroad
before six o'clock shadows fall

and night inks brick backways curving
through spiking garden hideouts.

Ticklish to the sun, tight-lipped
bulbs open into cups penciled

purple and edged frosty white,
center bursting with saffron fringes;

twigs snap like ancient wrist bones
as I sink down to crocus drifts—

swept in the frisson of wild beasts
and shoe-level color roars.

Detached

"Nobody reads anymore," says my editor,
"so find the story in the photo and fit the caption."
But twenty years after our last talk, you read
something I wrote before the erasure of stories
longer than a page, and we pick up our conversation
in the safety of distance and middle age—the wild
briar rose left to stale anthologies—and allow
"a life in letters" (despite keyboard taps finishing off
the ritual of stamps, ink, custom notecards),
and you invite me into buried stories:

your office window picturing your straight-line tale,
an everyday map locating secure bearings—
live oaks cooling salt-dome upheaval,
the commute of right angles and stoplight seething,
the college that buried you in seductive words,
the ancient cemetery desired by your urn . . .

the boyish big bang you got instead of star journeys,
a friend's accidental seven-iron swing to your skull,
flashes of red-yellow-blue spectrum explosions.
Ripped from its wall, your blood-rich left retina
drowned in poisonous fluid, like a ghost planet,
fading to brown-purple and streaking milky pink . . .

tales of croquet season, spring to October,
the pleasure of whites reflecting midsummer heat,
the self-labeled Cyclops lining up a shot,
robbed of depth perception and the truth of what's there,
still obsessed to lower your handicap
below 3.5 before another decade wanes . . .

late-night emails that open your back gate,
announcing the triumph of root stimulator
and the weight of budded roses, fringe tree blossoms
fleecing the air, Queen Anne's lace left unmown,
and I paint this verbal abandon, the lawn
pixelating from blue to green to purple . . .

yet the one time we meet in the accident
of daylight, your left iris freezes, windowless
to my heat-tipped fingers flirting inches away
while your right eye frames me out of the view.

Before Dogwood Winter

A storm lumbers and rolls,
like an animal turning
out of a long sleep,
and rain slashing at the skylight
nerves my fingers to frenzy
a canvas with a palette knife—
uncalculated motion
like the knowing that pushed
a rat snake from flooded
recesses to drape the stair
rail in a loopy figure eight.

I take brash stabs
at jonquils blaring
citron and tangerine,
stroke Lenten roses
dipping like parasols,
and daub saucer magnolia
goblets bobbling pink—
and I'm tipsy to tuck
a candy-striped camellia
in my hair before the outburst
of skin sheds and dogwood winter.

Death on a Sidewalk

I took a turn under a luncheon sun
for the unfurling of bearded iris flags,
billows unwound from pencil-thin buds—
purple, violet, blue, and cream petals
that I puddled and floated
on an archival page
in a class of middling women
lost in the paint-night spills
of dry rosé and gossip,
rendering watery Cotswold gardens,
masterworks to lavish on mudroom walls.

Yesterday a bed-edge iris took an early fall,
death by a rude shoe or tossed ball.
I stood over this rainbow rider,
dirt-bound and brick-baked,
its frills shriveling into bruises,
and yellowing, like the nicotine fingers
of my painting teacher
always tapping a Marlboro pack.

The iris cast a hard-headed silhouette
on the sidewalk—a gap in the ruffles,
like a jaw jutted open, in the moment of no air.

Never a Moonlit Lie

In the a.m. of my p.m., I stay
a sweet bay magnolia blossom,

like a tilt-a-whirl in the cup
of my hand, its spoon petals

deep enough to scoop last night's takeout—
wonton soup, now garbage to go.

Memorial Day never passed
without my mother's repeating

her hand-me-down design
of waxy ornamentals thrust

into tarnished trophy cups
and nicked Revere bowls

staggered on the mantel,
an altar of lemony intoxication

until veins crackled across
leaves curling brown

and blooms dimpled yellow,
like her thighs, and now mine;

the skin tells the sun's truth—
never a moonlit lie.

My Father on D-Day and Mountain Shade

They said the LST rode higher
in the water when landing in trim,

and on a stomach-churning morning,
she hit the beach slope; the bow door fell,

disgorging jeeps and tanks and finally us;
it was gray all around—the water, the sky,

the ships, as far as I could see, the one time
I looked back, and then only forward.

They made movies of our memories,
of what they thought they were:

German mortar and exploding artillery,
the strewn wreckage of flipped, ripped jeeps,

of wire, of bodies, whole, some with faces yet,
of twitching pieces, arms here and legs flung there,

of middle parts oozing guts—the sea foams,
so does blood. Then my hands did the thinking,

and doing, on semi-automatic,
what the doctor ordered: stanch bleeding,

apply dressings, sprinkle sulfa powder
(the lone wound antiseptic), and dwindle

the morphine on who has the best chance;
the hands became the machine that patched

the broken living, passing them to other hands
that stretchered them up the ramp.

I paused later—at the strangeness of it all.
Why Omaha? A city in a golden-prairie ocean.

Why Utah? A landlocked state with a salt lake.
But this Omaha, this Utah, opened to a dead sea,

where boys stepped off Higgins boats
and sank, murdered by their gear.

I saw, in a blind moment,
north Georgia mountain shade—

and tulip poplars growing straight,
reliably, their futures in coffins.

"Their wood is best," said Lem Moss, maker
of final boxes, "fast growing and long-lived."

When did coffins become caskets?
"Jewelry is for caskets," said my mother,

midwife and layer out of the dead,
giving up a bedsheet to line

somebody else's sleep, east-facing,
because that's the way it was always done.

She held them at their beginning,
and at their end—I was the lucky one,

finally home, for that long in between
when she held me in the mountain shade

one more time, many times over:
the boy, the man, the graying son.

Summer

Swimming After Trout

The sun prickles me,
and the dock creaks, rocking
on algae-spotted Styrofoam.
A silvery leap spatters
this drowsy morning,
now tail-thrashed alert
as trout flee weed beds
and sunken logs
for spring-fed depths—
far from the snaking neck
and strut and stalk
of a great blue heron.

My toes line the edge
of wave-slapped wood,
and I dive, in an arc,
into the current,
plunging below
tepid-safe waters,
desiring mute green
until the cool presses
hard on my breast,
and I push upward,
bursting into air,
a gasp of joy.

Central Florida Postcard

A crotch rocket muscles a GTO
and shoots into a tar-scorched mirage
far from city-center splendor
where fountains spritz,
arcing in pink-and-yellow play.

The rider leans hard,
hair stringing; her jean-tugged
butterfly peeps and spreads,
a purple-green mosaic
scaling butternut skin.

Stump pines rag the sky
great with rain, and light splits
heaven's underbelly;
God's fingers plume, fumbling
for Adam, but he's not there.

Chattahoochee: Songs I Never Heard till Now

The rush of I-285 sweeps me awake,
like the interior call of a conch shell

with a dry ocean trapped in its pink chamber,
and I retreat to the Chattahoochee,

hidden from Atlanta traffic lurching forward,
groan by groan, in the idling afternoon—

beyond apartments stacked like rabbit warrens
and the blue glow of bars where the nameless,

hunched over phones, munch pretzels and reach
for mint mojitos sugar-muddling Saturday.

On Powers Island, a fisherman, with name
and number Sharpie-scrawled on his life vest,

launches a rowboat in the easy pull
to drift behind a tuber flotilla;

I dabble my feet by a lichen-bearded log
heard by Canada geese on its bank-hollowing fall.

The sun slaps eddies, and brown-gray plumage
runs in short currents on a gander that hooks

his beak in a ripple, stabbing and nibbling,
then arching and shooting up his neck,

mate alert—his white cheek patches, like arrows,
paint his ebony head and crown.

I draw a sharp breath, rocked by the grace
of a flock, heads erect, paddling sideways

and honking, tugged southward, and mourn
the questions never asked of my mother:

Did you paddle the river and cast long,
slow-motion lines—ambitionless to net

a mess of sun-flashed rainbow trout?
You, the dreamer, whose river fortune

I never knew, what tunes did you hum
to bankside gurgles and midstream rapids?

Coneflower Sequence

Last spring, I wanted something trouble-free
and found it in coneflower seed packets,
buying into the midsummer promise
of self-sowing sun lovers—now overrunning
the garden with nature's lavender turns.
Seed heads bristle symmetry, measure
upon measure, Fibonacci's weathered tune
luring goldfinches to August feasts.

Peach Heat: Out of Hand

In the burn of summer,
we swiped peaches
along a two-lane road
in Chilton County.
I picked the first,
heavy with juice
and russet-pink-orange,
like a sunset haze,
that I dropped in his palm.
His thumb ran along
the cleft, then he bit
the velvet skin and reached
in for the stone, saying,
"Nothing like cling-free,"
and tossed it.

Deception

He painted promises,
the ever turn of Earth
shimmering on an oak panel:
emerald and terracotta
floating on marine blue swathed
in swirls, night edging
out day and cities winking
like electric constellations.

He wrote love songs
to the shape-shifter moon:
a disk in shadow
an ashen diadem
an ochre quarter
a creamy globe
a low-hung lamp
over ripe fields.

He handed me both worlds,
like borosilicate marbles,
but I lost them to what is:
no breeze, no rain
to salve meteor pocks,
the moon hangs,
a frigid nightlight
pulling at Earth;
waters bulge and crash,
while Earth fixates
on arid basins,
raising crusty tides.

Nowhere Duet

Shivers stole over me as fingers slid along the curve of my neck and squeezed my clavicle, playing me for a fool, and I swayed into his embrace.

Our tango whirled night into day, running down the clocks. His sweaty hand caught my raised wrist, and I faced him, fighting for breath. Dry lips parted, I drew closer, lured by a straining violin.

I kicked up dust from heart-pine boards and wrapped my leg around his thigh; blood-rush dips intoxicated, but his grip slackened, and I crashed, a dime-a-dance girl, desperate for the box step of a metronome life.

He hibernated until forsythia stars exploded and grape hyacinths massed in low beds. He slipped his foot just inside the slam of my door, and his shoes drummed as an ancient tamburello shook.

He knelt briefly, then galloped three steps, and his left foot tripped me. Pawing his left hand, he gamboled three steps ahead, turned, sprang, and bit. The sting of ritual poison sent waves up my legs in 6/8 rhythm.

Iron notes skittered along my spine until a repeat Middle C marched me out the door as mop-headed hydrangeas pelted the lawn blue.

The Shadow of My Father's Beard

My father's beard bristled my cheek at 5 a.m.
while my mother lilted, "Rise and shine," in the dark
of day number four for child number four to fish
with the week's ruler of a 100-acre Florida lake,
a hot field of lily pads floating on water as dark
as ripened plums—where Old Granddaddy lurked,
king of a mythic domain beyond taxonomic rank.

I preferred picking water lilies to plumbing
the depths for a ghost, but my father side-pinched
a cricket between his thumb and pointer finger,
stuck the hook, in the back, just behind the head,
and threaded it—the legs churned, and I looked away,
slapping at gnats that weren't there.

Shoved in the shade of the boat's middle seat,
the cricket box stayed mute. (Did they know?)
The cork float bobbed, sleep-blurring the pole
out of my hands, and my father grabbed it;
I looked down, pulling hard on the turquoise ribbons
of my mother's straw hat until the brim flattened
on either side of my head, like folded wings.

He pan-fried supper and showed us
how to bite the tip of a crisp bream tail
dotted with salt and peppery cornmeal.
The porch song wore down
as the cricket box emptied; the last of them clung,
for no reason, to the fine wire mesh.
My father iced and packed headless fish,
silver-clean and fin-stiff, in his metal chest:
home-bound treasure for the freezer.

At 5 a.m. today, a lone cricket's chirp
stop-started, like a song skipping on vinyl,
and boxed me in, irked, until I passed my hands,
moist with coconut oil and sweat, over my face—
the faint scent of Florida and the summer

of seersucker over blouses and Peter Pan collars
and shorts with grown-up back zippers,
and my father reaching out to pluck a pale lily,
out of purple water, just for me.

Immersion

I would never toe-squish into a river
just to salvage my muddy, sidestepping soul—

the sun's fire plunges me into a gunite pool
rimmed with turquoise tiles. Paced by flutter kicks

and concrete-grazed flip turns, my meditation runs
long and lean, a state of grace fogging my goggles

as my thoughts slow in cloudy sounds and disappear
into my paint-box season of sea-salt breezes

and the Gulf of Mexico swelling Veronese green.
Waves break, seafoam like linen cambric, rushing

toward a dome house shaped after my mother showed me
how to dig my foot in the sand and hold it there,

while my hands patted a dwelling that God
would not understand—more than something

built on a rock when decorated with coquina
butterflies gathered when we trailed their swash-zone flights.

Scooped and tossed with the swipe of each wave,
the tinier-than-penny shells ripple rainbows,

sunsets, and indigo depths, a bucketful
of wonders finer than my fingerprints—

I hear summer squeaks in a thousand footfalls
denting chalk-white dunes until popping up

for breath in the chlorine squeals of children
water-winging in the pool's shallows.

Summer Contained

In-and-out shadow clouds press morning air,
squeezing the sweet odor of a storm
heavy with August plant oils and earth.
They buried my mother in blue—I forgot
to ask which shade; cornflower or robin's egg
or teal would have been nice, but a bird strike
delayed the plane, and I was too late to look.

I turn the spade, committing an urn
of lemon balm to a casual death,
and fill in my mother's paint-by-number
September of purple kale center drama,
johnny jump-ups, and blueberry thrill pansies—
the season that slipped away when she forgot
how to swallow vanilla custard ice cream.

Fall

Opening to Your Dark Eye

The electricity buzzed out,
extinguishing the dinner party;
my mother sighed over table elbows,
hurried dinners, and napkins tossed
aside on plates dribbled with gravy—
resuscitating an Emily Post adage:
"Etiquette is the science of living."
She died. What did it matter?

I divorced embossed stationery
and sold the Steuben candlesticks,
each teardrop base entrapping
the shape of a Hershey kiss—
like a bell that would never ring
in chilly air (glass in its molten state
resembles the final design, a moment
frozen from process, said the maker).

The movers shattered my collection
of blue Haviland porcelain,
and I caved to dining with the dimmer
turned down and thought spelunking,
caught in the tale of your eye blinded
by the errant swing of a golf club,
and your confession that was the one place
you could hold me, without straying.

Royal Wind Riders

A biology teacher dispatched me to collect
insect quarry in September's fading days,

and I waited out a chrysalis until it cracked,
a wet crumple clinging to the shell

as I hovered with a quick lid and a Mason jar
fuming with a splash of rubbing alcohol.

The monarch's wings dried, spreading until I scooped
it to murder within three desperate flaps,

denying the rule driven by one design—
a never-ceasing line of four generations,

like solar flares, spent spring into summer,
fluttering one month toward inglorious death

except for the season's final heirs—migrants
beating to coastal California and Mexico

at the whim of high winds until dropping
to roost on trees, hanging like tiger-stripe curtains,

warming until their rides on upward air
to bask in the sun beyond binocular view.

I, the prisoner of a GPS, wonder
at their return, thousands of miles, to pair off

in early spring; their eggs, like periods,
punctuate the underside of milkweed leaves.

The caterpillars hatch and gnaw, shedding
five times over, until crawling off to digest

their rippled bodies, dissolving in soup
cocooned in cases like gold-speckled jade—

awakening, fewer each year, outnumbered
by Starbucks in Golden State winters,

their day of the dead repeating, season-long,
with Midwest milkweed succumbing to herbicide

and nectar flowers wasted by insecticides
intended for moths, mosquitos, grasshoppers.

The legend—the flight of souls, each less
than a gram—fades the way of passenger pigeons

that smothered skies but disappeared in fifty years.
Freeing a butterfly releases a divine wish—

but that old tale escaped me a half-century ago
when I lost my way, snuffing out a jewel.

The New Orange

In the dead of August, yellowing leaves scuttle Alabama yards unready for rakes—autumn's casual brush-by, a 68-degree flirt with sweater weather after a fine rain. In a deeper south, the Amazon burns; the slideshow plays a frame or two on a small screen until swiped by android thumbs tracking the points of the Dow jagging red.

Rainforest palms fan their last against dusky pumpkin skies—"smelling like barbecue," say journalists. "What?" wonder the casual. "The whole hog pit-roasted over hickory and drizzled with vinegar? Mustard and paprika-heated dry rub powdered with garlic, brown sugar, and allspice? Smoked chicken sweating peppery mayonnaise?"

Ceramic tile chills my feet, and I grope for an orange shrinking in the refrigerator bin. Memory peels back to frosty mornings when I rode with my father to the farmers market in Birmingham's West End. Fires burned in rusting drums, and we huddled, waiting for citrus hauled from groves where seasons went green year-round.

Blast furnaces cast a tangerine glow until dawn streaked, and the sun flashed rigs bearing exotics with names to dream on. Valencia, Indian River, Satsuma, and Seville took the choke out of those sulfur days, the never-letup of iron-smelting. Now he's gone. The forests are going. We arrive—where nothing ambrosial stays.

Around the Corner

David and Danny stray from Farmer Brown's field,
following its creek in search of mysteries

when something scuttles in the shallows, pinching
and pleasing. "What is it?" whispers David.

"A fish, a crawling fish," says Danny, folding
on his knees at the bank's edge and stretching out

his hand, then hesitating, frightened at the pincers
but thrilled to the shell, thick and calcified.

"Why is it?" whispers David, and Danny hovers
his fingers over the water, just an inch,

and glimpses the broken joint of a missing leg
before rapid tail flips jerk the creature backward.

At five, he's out of words, agitated by the heat
and the racket of cicadas buzzing

and clicking their last month high in the trees
after shedding years burrowed below.

At dusk, the crickets start their tinny chirrs,
between the whines of katy-did-katy-didn't,

and tree frogs throw trills like ventriloquists,
calling out thunderstorms in steamy air—

night vibrating against the screens,
Danny forgets how his father sounded,

losing one more piece to a summer hollowed
like cicada husks littering the ground.

At thirty-five, he overhears retired guys
in a diner, sipping coffee and devouring

Danish while they recite obituaries
that praise fruitful years (or mask wasted days)

and sigh, "I had no idea so-and-so was sick."
But he's too hurried for capsule biographies

of politicians and poets, teachers
and engineers, CEOs and truck drivers,

because fall cleanup is overdue since the cold
silenced the nights, and he cannot put off

patching bald spots and mulching perennials;
the checklist is longer than he'd like to think.

Danny goes around the corner of the house
to grab a rake; his son rattles the playpen,

pulling up to find his feet—his eyes grip the sky,
full of cloud rollovers, as Danny returns, glancing

sideways, at his father's black hair, an instant,
like the crawfish dart, while his son yearns upward.

Apple Chill

Orchard branches gnarled,
I picked an apple,
sepia-grained red,
and cut into the flesh—
the seed-dimpled slice
tartly chilled my mouth.

The quarter horse
nuzzled yellow grass
and nibbled his fill
of bruised ripening,
lips velvet and damp,
and it was enough.

Blue Ridge Weather Report

Canada comes, you announce, cooling
the Blue Ridge in chlorophyll-starved
splendor, blazing sourwood and black gum,
yellowing hickories and tulip trees,
dashing maroon and russet on oaks,
firing orange across sassafras.

Umber splotches rosy dogwood leaves,
and birds snatch at candy-berry clusters
while the morning moon burns white in blue.
My face upturns to catch the sun's glow
through lidded eyes as the wind stirs limbs,
dropping leaves, and I report dry rain.

Frost pales the trees and thins chirping,
whirring call-and-response night song.
I grieve the rasping choir without you,
look for the farmer's geese, snowy flecks
in a browning yard, but he has sold them,
and the gate squeaks, half-open.

October Martini

Sunlight slants, stingy at 6 p.m.; in November,
I will fall back for an extra hour of shadow,

a false gain against the loss of afternoon gold
with contrails etching and fraying against azure.

The furor of summer buzz dissipated to a hum,
a bee dances with a magenta rugosa rose

grabbing hold of anthers, clutching at one more hour,
like the day I hung on to your words that calmed

my computer clacking—as if my hands hit spectral notes,
rhythms halting until your right hand took

the middle voice and your left, the bass, tempering
flails at trills and dots, stepping down from F-sharp minor.

Faithful in our fashion, we move with a carefulness,
like the way you measure gin from a sapphire bottle,

kissing it with vermouth and two drops of orange bitters;
we pause for the long-distance click of frosted glasses,

October moistening our lips and your eyes flecking
gold, brown, and rainy, like an ambiguous autumn

in Mississippi—nature has a way of turning
parlor tricks: the heartline forks in my right palm.

Persimmon Surrender

Persimmons hang like paper-lantern globes
on branches pronging hard-frost skies—
I pluck the first, and cinnamon flesh
shrivels under my fingers.

I remember not to swallow the seeds,
long oval and flat, shaped like the mirror
cracked by my fist when Mom disappeared
with the car keys and forgot her address.

Autumn Coda, Winter Wondering

You, the teacher, unbolted a library
laden with human noise bound in leather
and cracked open an eye slit of nature:
the limping hare, the iron-cold owl,
the wounded goose's blood drops
sinking fast into crusted snow.

Now you push me out the door
to travel, widely, within one mile,
the Chattahoochee's moods.
The sun, November spent, flicks
at cayenne-and-cumin scatterings
along the river road, while leaves
cling, backlit and oxblood red,
on gray knuckles and joints.

I skip the florist for the forest floor,
gathering wilderness decorations
through the holidays: loblolly pines,
with plated trunks like the chipped
beards and locks of Sumerian kings,
fling palm-pricking pyramid cones
and evergreen brooms; raindrops tear
on nandina berries glowing toxic red.

The swamp, to the west, sleeps,
lulled by mists and tree-slogged soils,
until a mallard pokes the tail feathers
of his mate, rippling the pool.
She scoots and then preens
before tipping forward to graze;
she pops up, bobbing, feathers
patterned like bridal-hennaed hands.

Leaning into this new-year nursery,
I know your blessing.

The Fifth Season

Birdwatch

Everything came sooner that year—
'February Gold' daffodils frilling
the neighbor's yard, marching in patches,
like bonneted Dutch dolls on the quilts
hand-stitched by my grandmother in the halo
of a Depression glass kerosene lamp;
the ground thaw of the full worm supermoon,
with the mounding of earthworm droppings
crushed under my boot weeks
before the tropical rush of stopover warblers;
March passing, blurred with rain and dark clumps
of turkey vultures roosting in a stand
of loblolly pines—I sheltered in place,
exceeding social distancing by a backyard length,
in full retreat to an afternoon of porch sitting—
weary of text bursts and COVID-19 tweetstorms.

I heard hissing, and my neighbor, fenced in,
called that the birds would not snatch the pacing cat.
I took up my father's cracked binoculars,
trying to zero in, for the first time, on why
he hovered over field guides to American birds;
his lifelong dream was to find a birdfeeder
that defied squirrels—he never did.
The vultures' red, shrunken heads wrinkled,
scrubbed bald, like the scalps of monks;
the night before, their hooked beaks, like polished bone,
had ripped into a possum rotting by the garbage.
Free of flesh, they flapped, shaking off the damp,
and rose, thermal riding, with the two-tone underside
of their wings spread in shallow V's—carrion-feaster comfort
wing-warping on a cleansing breeze.

Song on a Winter's Day

"Did I mention I do not like February?" you text,
short on words in the shortest month of the year

and voyage toward a far country, shut in your library,
leaving me behind in the emptiness of here,

wondering where the years take us, mild flirtations
intertwining with tender ailments—the dentist

digging out thirty-year fillings, sunrise twinges
in the low back, the greening of your croquet days

in the rearview mirror, the passport photo that may be
my last, the joke we are finally our parents' age.

Byzantium becomes yours on this black-ice night,
but I clutch your notes ripped from a legal pad,

where you wrote of craving eight-hour sunlight
in the bare season of your rose sanctuary—

the days of clippers and gloves, of cutting out
deadwood and crossing branches, of sculpting

the cane shape for mid-spring's fever flush;
you're not out of nature yet: every Friday,

you savor whisky's sway—the swirls and pull-down
drips in the glass, like Romanesque windows,

flickering copper to mahogany and the whiffs
into tastemaker memory—dried fruit, chocolate,

the spice of a girl's lipstick when you kissed her
on your college break, in the rustle of corn before it tasseled.

As sure as the gargle and roll of whisky around your mouth,
and the burn of a long finish, vernal rains will spatter

this skeleton month, with moonlit hares drawing out snowy owls
and the sun fielding daffodil galaxies, and we will hold on,

adding days to life's brief sum before surrendering
to the glitter of tesserae seas and gold-hammered birds.

When You Need a Chat with Jesus

"Four errands and enervated," you text
just before Holy Week. "Tire store, market,
pharmacy, and the Episcopal church
to invest in the columbarium niche

for our ashes ... I need a chat with Jesus."
That's a first, I think, recalling your devotion
to the Magdalene, the no-doubt
apostle abiding at the cross and tomb.

But now her chiaroscuro portrait (hair
like sand waves rippling Monument Valley
and the skull in her lap with sockets
like asphalt-patched potholes) cracks in the glare

of your caregiving, the 24/7
intimacy known only to the spouse
remembering and the beloved forgetting.
Your dispatches curtail as days fracture

into chores: tightening the toilet seat,
kneeling to scrub, carpentering a rail
to ease steps to the driveway, stripping sheets,
counting out meds for the pillbox—

reminders of my father's bucket list,
shrunken to odd jobs, conversation reruns,
my mother singing snatches of swing tunes
and the hymn refrain about a wildwood church.

I imagine your reading stories aloud
to your wife, getting lost in neighborhoods
that mapped early arrivals—hints of peach
and apricot floating above tea olive trees,

the aroma mélange block after block ...
cayenne, paprika, cumin, garlic, coffee,
tobacco, incense, the holy trinity
of onion, celery, bell pepper sweating in butter ...

How long do words hold when the oldest sense,
the retriever of autobiography, departs,
memory muddied, as if carried away
by the Mississippi picking up silt, sand, clay?

When you're done and sore and grief spent,
and Melville's cry—"Oh Time, Strength, Cash,
and Patience!"—no longer serves, you admit
you're a christian (emphasizing "little c").

That's the comforter's cue to roll in for cocktails,
a no-fuss guy like the limewood sculpture
astride a bowed donkey on braced legs pulled
along by medieval crowds in Palm Sunday parades.

This Jesus, expecting nothing, is fine
sitting down for an heirloom tomato sandwich
swiped with twangy mayonnaise, a dram,
plus whatever else you might pour out.

what's more

white space
cuts lines—
our more

because less
is okay
nothing to read

between—
only what
we know

ut pictura poesis

watercolor
luminous
on cotton

white shape
an act
of exclusion

Queen of the Night
a torch
shooting flames

from Payne's gray
depths until doused
by dawn

our once-a-year
courtyard vigil—
brief candle out

but here
on this page
brief is always

all ours
whatever
the hour

At Sunrise: Metta Meditation

In stillness at sunrise,
I slide bloodstone beads

between my fingers,
counting nothing—

my hands, invisible to words,
shut out my mouth,

and I hear the songs you strummed
before giving away your Gibson—

my thoughts skim
your way, like a hummingbird,

the weight of a postage stamp,
dipping and cloud surfing

turquoise skies, her heart
electrifying a whir

on the easy breath
of the Gulf of Mexico:

may you be peaceful,
may you be well,

may you know emerald springs
and ruby-throated joy.

Acknowledgments

My thanks to the editors of the following publications and writing communities where these poems were first acknowledged, sometimes in different form.

Anacapa Review: "Opening to Your Dark Eye"

Appalachian Places: "Around the Corner" and "Swimming After Trout"

ArtAscent, Portraits Competition (Distinguished Writer): "The Shadow of My Father's Beard"

The Blue Mountain Review and Natasha Trethewey Poetry Prize (2020 runner-up): "2020 Birdwatch" (retitled "Birdwatch")

Braided Way Magazine: "At Sunrise: For My Teacher" (retitled "At Sunrise: Metta Meditation")

The Citron Review: "Deception"

Didcot Writers, Apple-Trees-Woodland Competition (Reader's Choice): "Apple Chill"

The Ekphrastic Review: "Death on a Sidewalk"

Eunoia Review: "Backyard Mardi Gras Baby" (retitled "Fat Tuesday Freeze"), "Central Florida Postcard," "Immersion," "Never a Moonlit Lie," "The New Orange," "Second Chance Crack-up," and "Through Irish Eyes"

Natasha Trethewey Poetry Prize (2024 runner-up): "Lithium Unplugged"

The Orchards Poetry Journal: "Iowa Dreams" and "Song on a Winter's Day"

Pine Mountain Sand & Gravel: "My Father on D-Day and Mountain Shade"

Pink Panther Magazine: "Origins of the World in a Greenhouse" and "Summer Contained"

The Poeming Pigeon: "Royal Wind Riders"

Sparks of Calliope: "Chattahoochee: Songs I Never Heard till Now"

storySouth: "Detached"

The Sunlight Press: "Crocus Drifts" (retitled "Fauve Crocuses")

Tiny Seed Journal: "Autumn Coda, Winter Wondering"

Vita Brevis: "Coneflower Sequence"

Willows Wept Review: "Blue Ridge Autumn" (retitled "Blue Ridge Weather Report") and "October Martini"

Winter 2020: Childhood: Vol. 1 (The Poet): "Origami Storm"

Profound gratitude to Madville Publishing director Kim Davis and poetry editor Linda Parsons for accepting and guiding this collection to its final form. Deepest thanks to author and illustrator Michael Austin and colleague Sharron Lehman for thoughtful comments and steadfast support through multiple revisions. Much appreciation to editor Joshua Wilson whose honest, insightful feedback pushed me to dig deeply and keep refining. A shoutout to the Atlanta Writers Club, especially board member Jerry Weiner and executive director George Weinstein, who manages the Atlanta Writers Conference and tirelessly advises members on the publishing industry.

Notes

"Night of the Insistent Moon": the phrase "there are tears in things" derives from the Latin phrase *sunt lacrimae rerum* from Book I, line 462 of *The Aeneid* by Virgil. Aeneas, defeated at Troy and far from his destroyed home, stops at a temple and weeps on seeing murals with scenes from the Trojan War, including images of dead friends and fellow citizens. Seamus Heaney's interpretation of Aeneas' explanation to a comrade—"there are tears at the heart of things"—speaks to the human capacity to know distress and sorrow while arriving at a place or condition of safety.

"Fauve Crocuses": the phrase "wild beasts" references Fauves, early 20th-century painters who used dabs of bold complementary color to create a visual "frisson."

"Song on a Winter's Day": the phrase "out of nature" is from William Butler Yeats' poem "Sailing to Byzantium," published in *The Tower* (1928). The phrase "gold-hammered birds" references lines in the fourth stanza: "a form as Grecian goldsmiths make / Of hammered gold and gold enamelling." The phrase "life's brief sum" references the title of Ernest Dowson's poem *Vitae summa brevis spem nos vetat incohare longam* ("The brief sum of life denies us the hope of enduring long"), borrowed from one of Horace's odes and published in *The Poems and Prose of Ernest Dowson* (1900).

About the Author

Catherine Hamrick started her career in print, working at *Southern Living, Cooking Light, Southern Accents, Victoria, Better Homes and Gardens,* and Meredith Books. She taught writing and communication arts at several colleges and universities before jumping into digital marketing as a copywriter and content strategist. Her poetry has appeared in *The Blue Mountain Review, Appalachian Places, Pine Mountain Sand & Gravel, storySouth, The Citron Review,* and elsewhere. She practices yoga, paints on occasion, and scribbles first drafts the old-fashioned way—in notebooks from discount stores. Find her online at catherinehamrick.com.